ACCENT ON THE
SEASONS

BY WILLIAM GILLOCK

12 ORIGINAL PIANO SOLOS

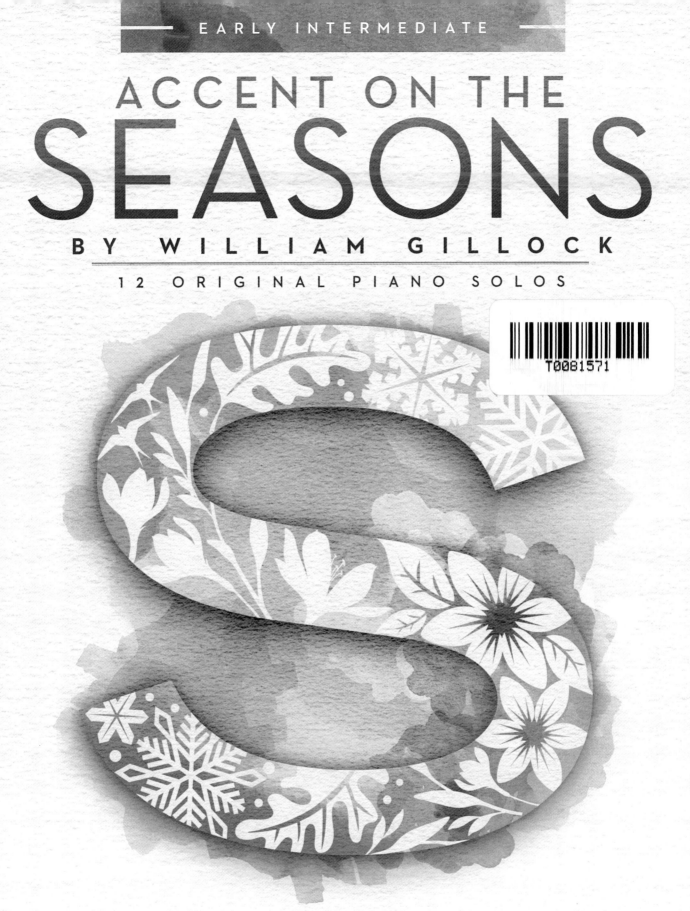

ISBN 978-1-4803-4072-5

EXCLUSIVELY DISTRIBUTED BY

WILLIS MUSIC

HAL•LEONARD®
CORPORATION
7777 W. BLUEMOUND RD. P.O. BOX 13819
MILWAUKEE, WISCONSIN 53213

Visit Hal Leonard Online at
www.halleonard.com

TO THE PERFORMER

Mr. Gillock intended the pieces in this book to be played at any time of the year! However, these pieces are also perfectly suitable for seasonal studio recitals and performances. A few may be interchangeable; for example, "Windy Weather" or "Horseback Ride." Enjoy!

CONTENTS

SUMMER

FALL

WINTER

SPRING

ACCENT ON THE
SEASONS

Summertime Blues

William Gillock

Slow Blues tempo

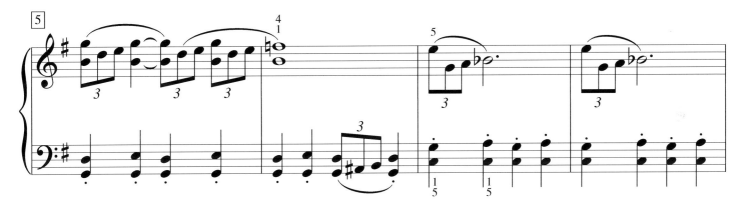

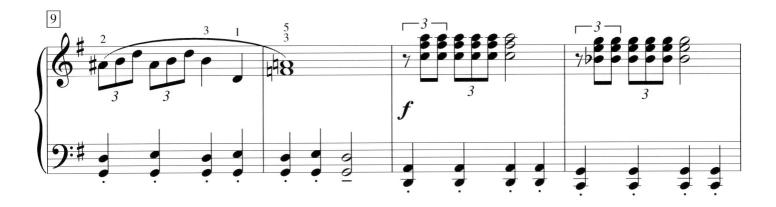

Horseback Ride

William Gillock

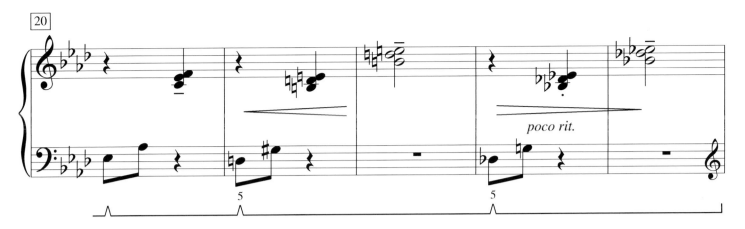

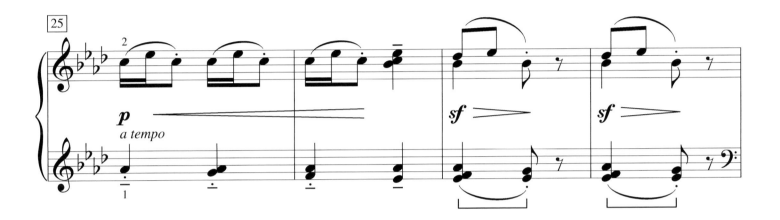

Summertime Caprice

William Gillock

In a flowing style

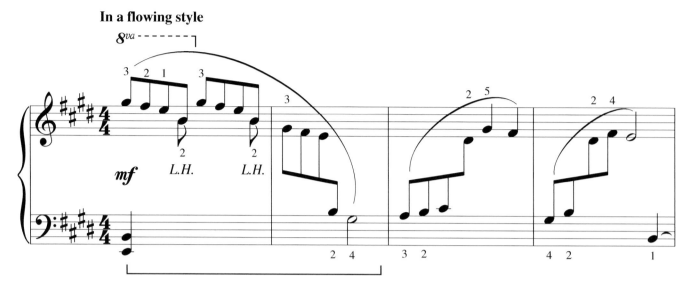

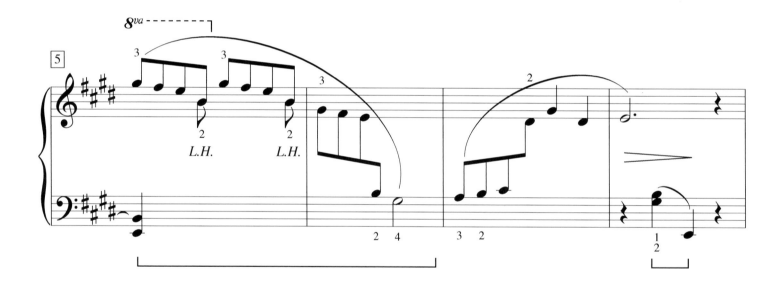

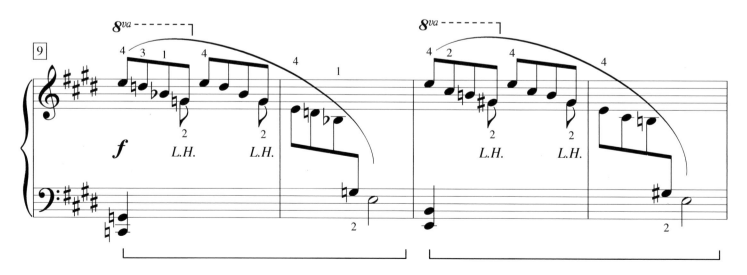

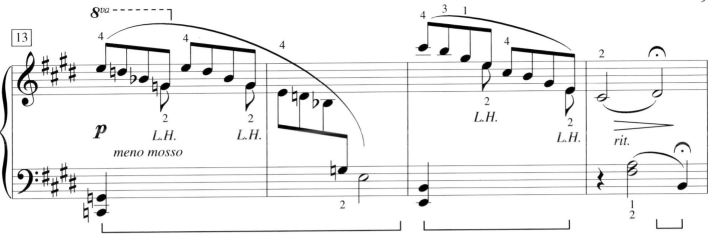

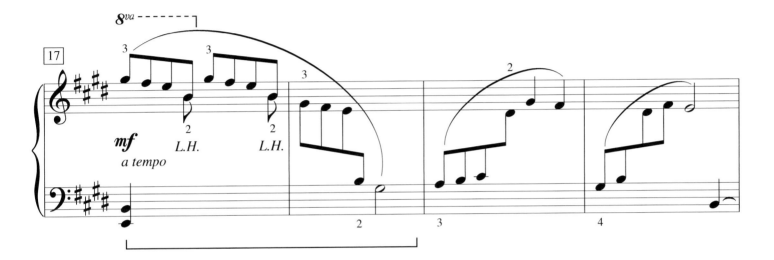

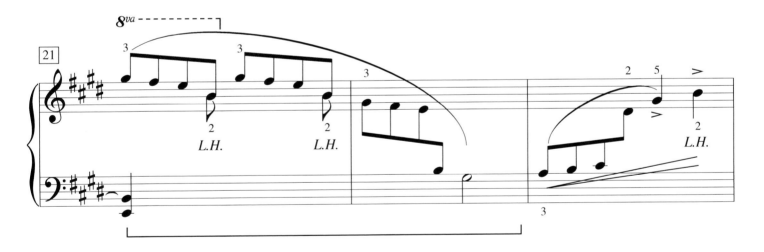

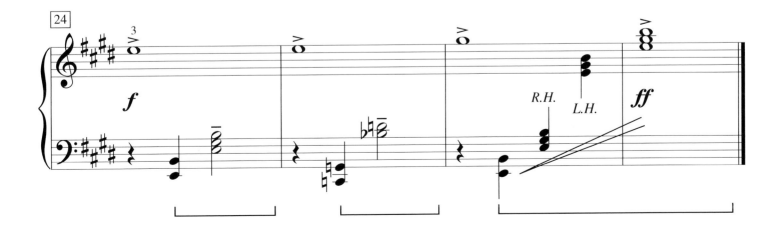

The Haunted Tree

William Gillock

Quick and mysterious

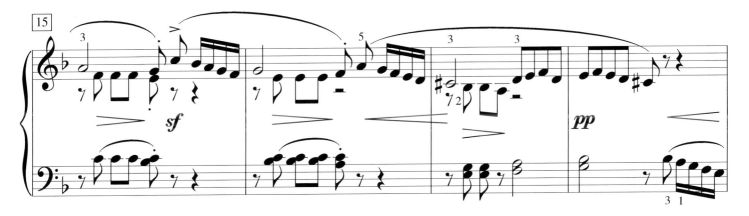

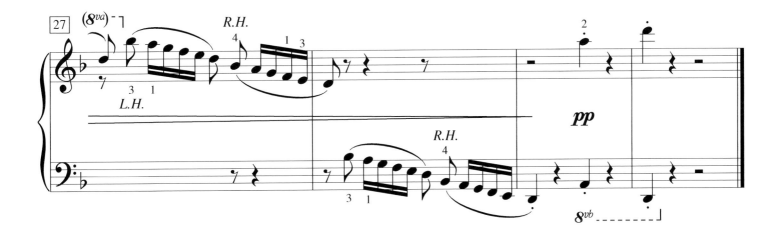

Waltz for Autumn

William Gillock

Slowly, always lingering

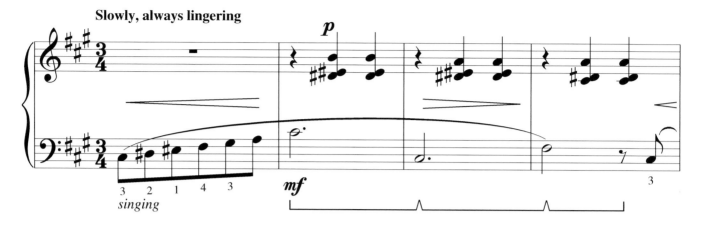

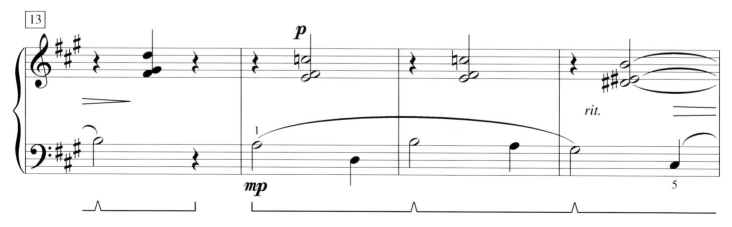

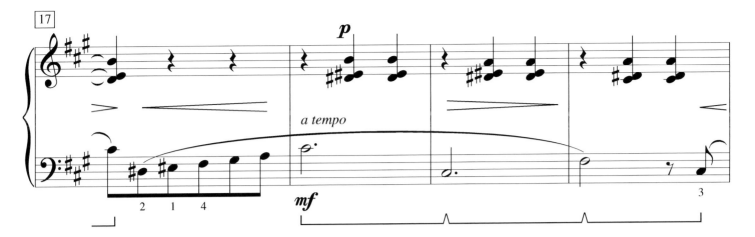

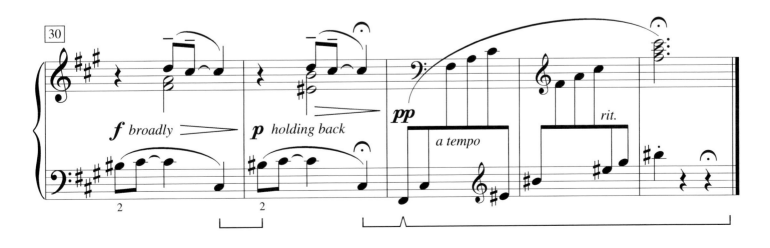

Journey in the Night

William Gillock

Allegro con brio

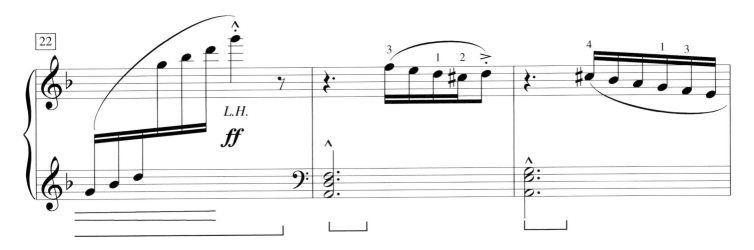

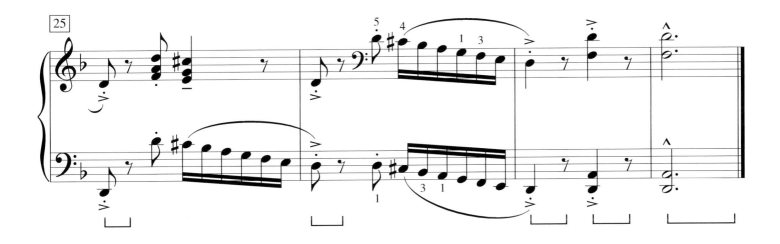

To Susan and Laura Earls

Figure Skating

William Gillock

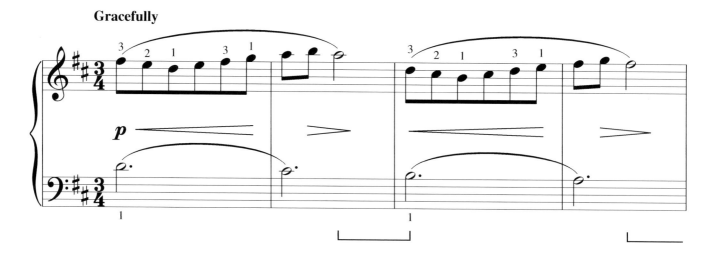

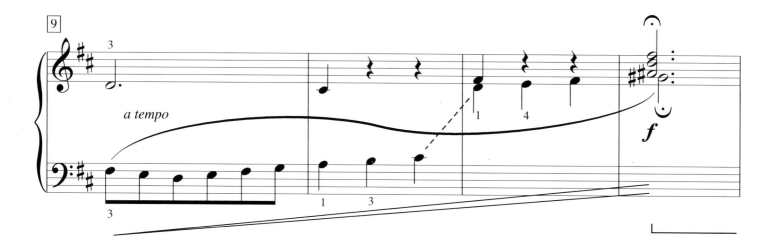

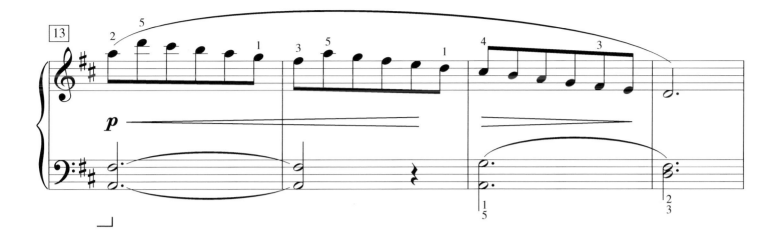

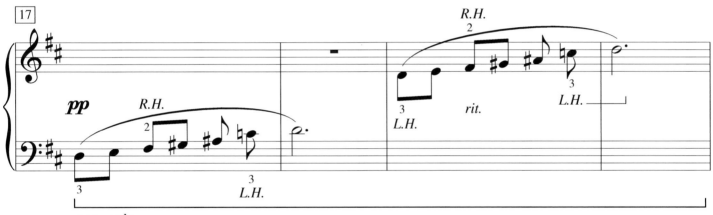

una corda

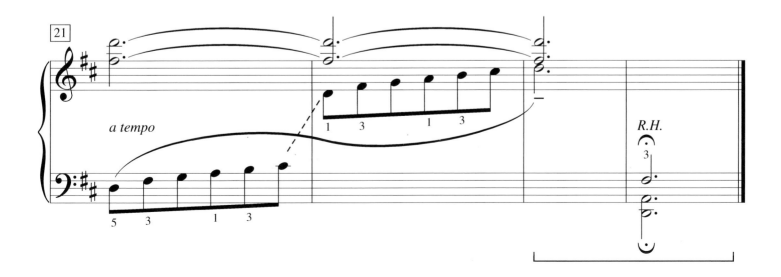

To James and Scott
Graceful Skiers

William Gillock

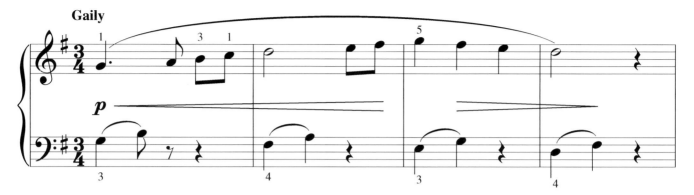

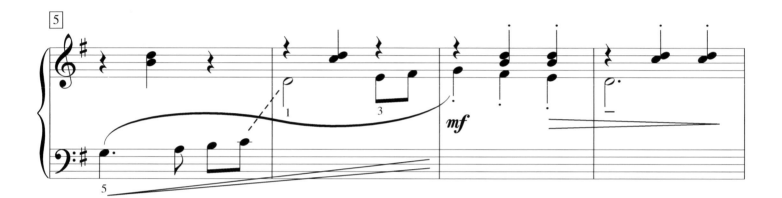

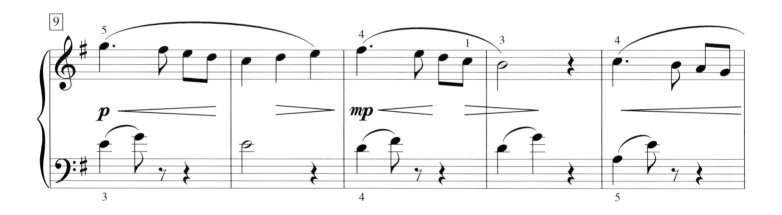

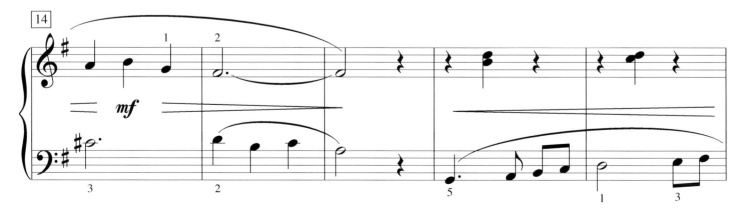

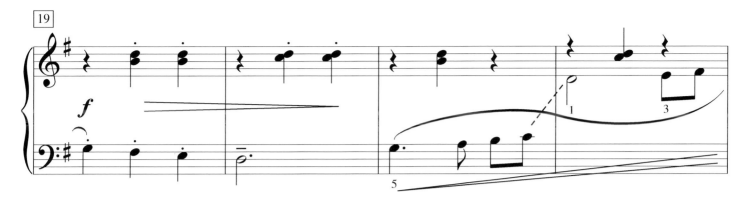

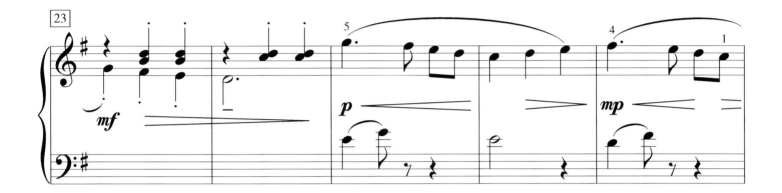

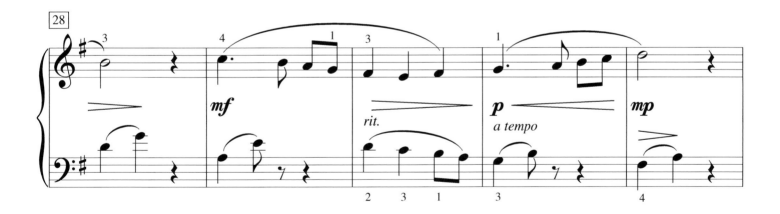

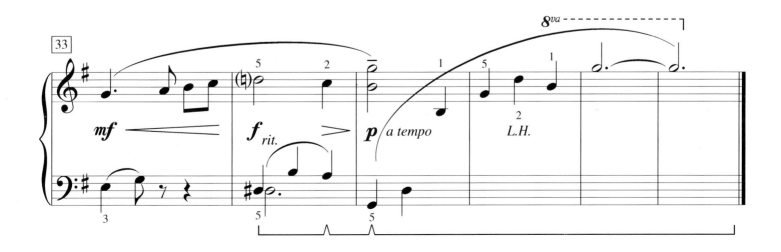

To Everett Stevens

Sleigh Ride

William Gillock

Swift and light

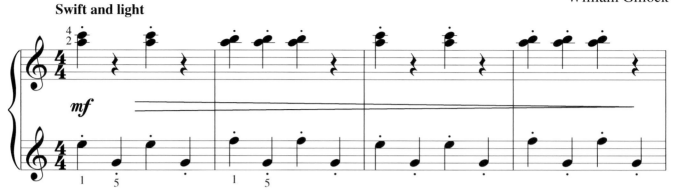

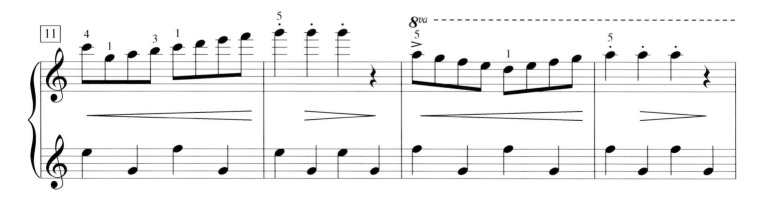

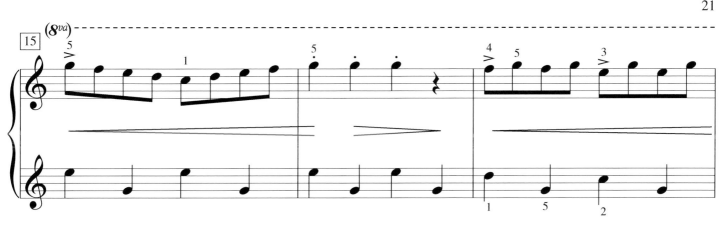

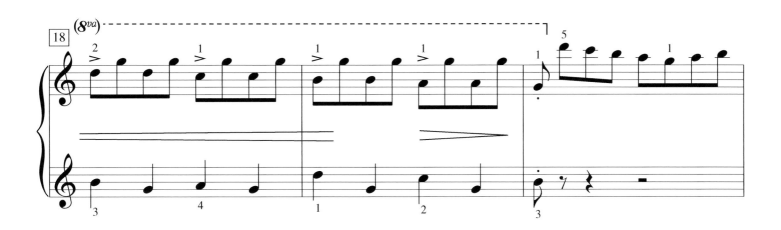

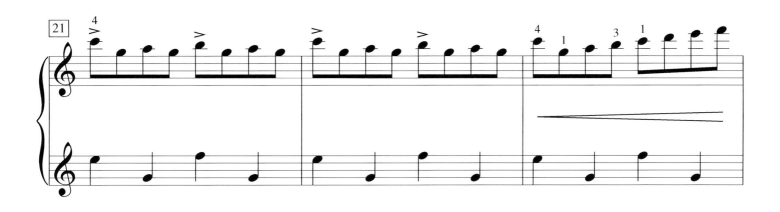

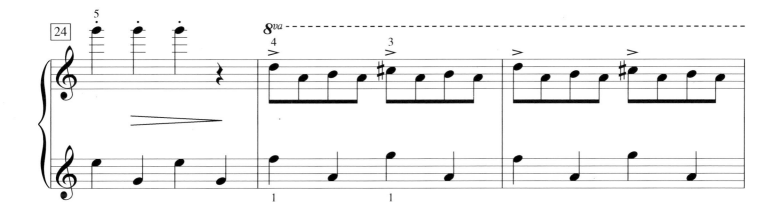

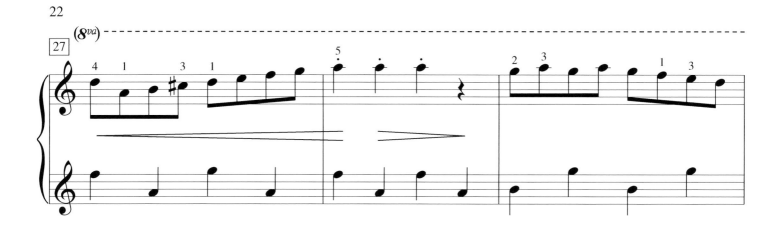

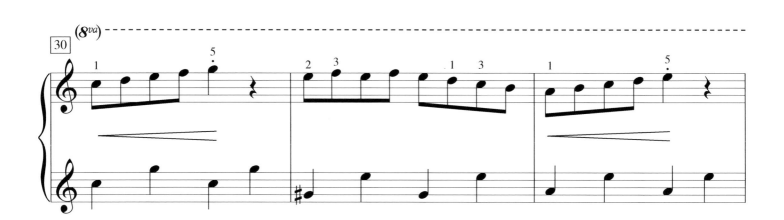

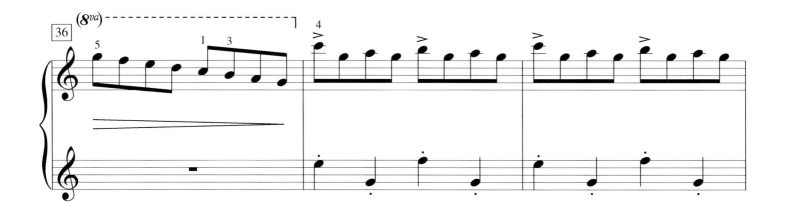

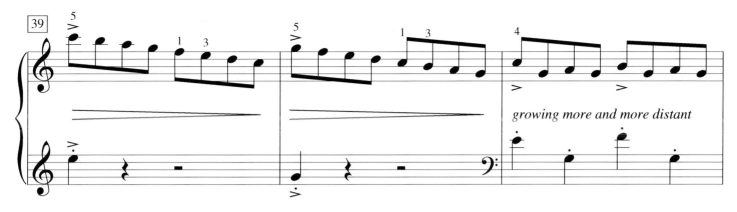

growing more and more distant

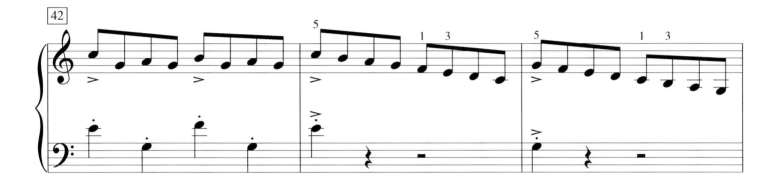

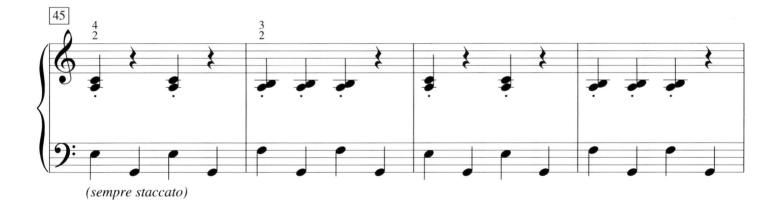

(sempre staccato)

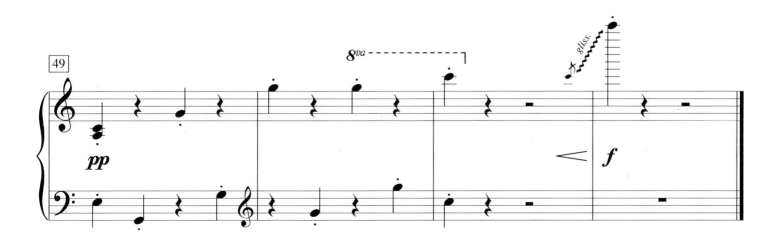

Windy Weather

William Gillock

Lively

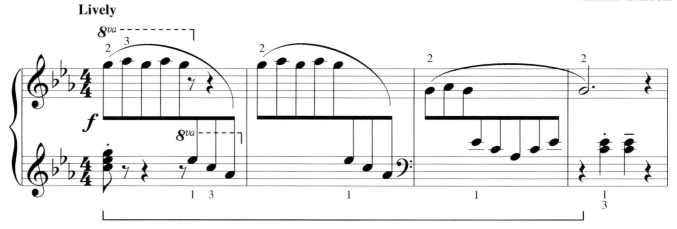

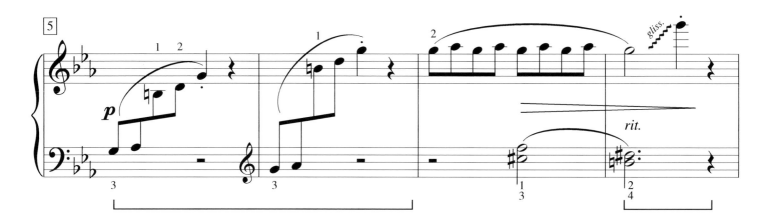

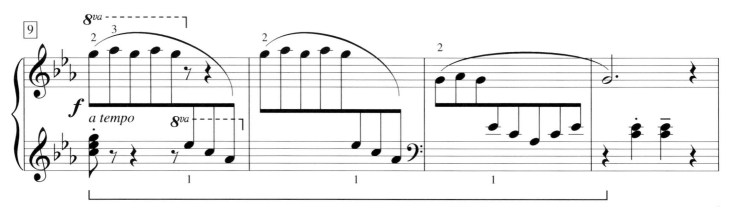

To Coda ⊕

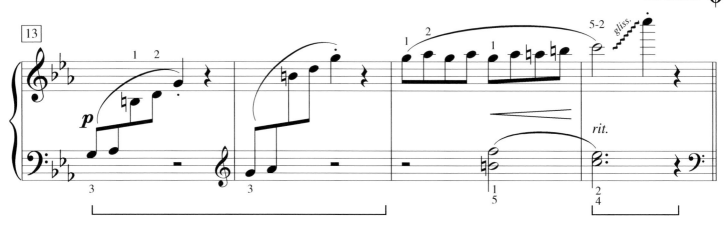

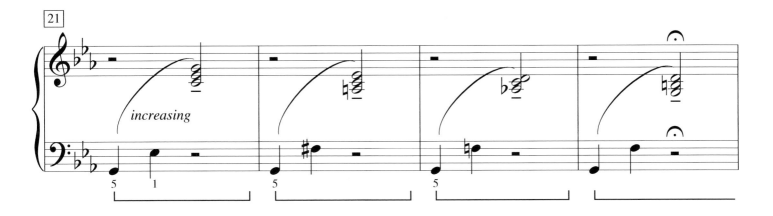

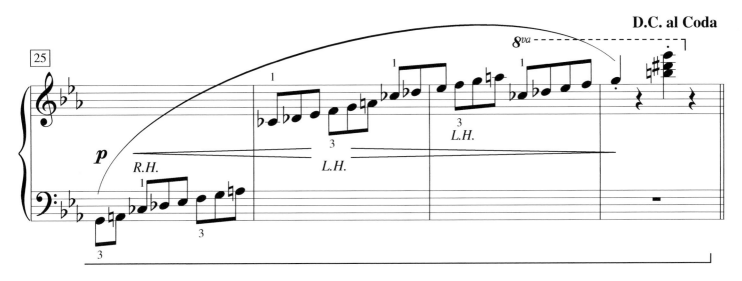

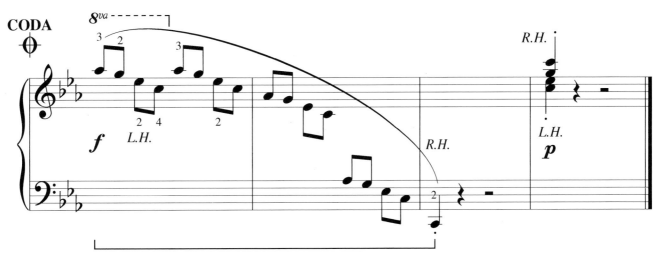

Dancing in the Garden

William Gillock

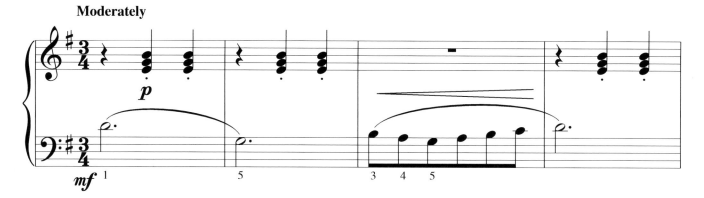

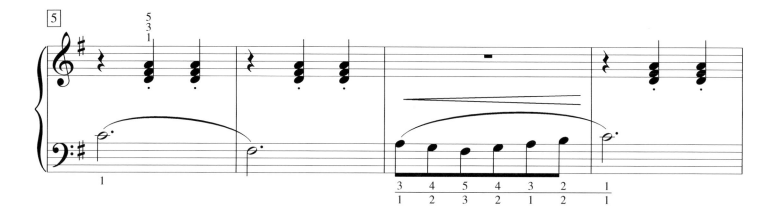

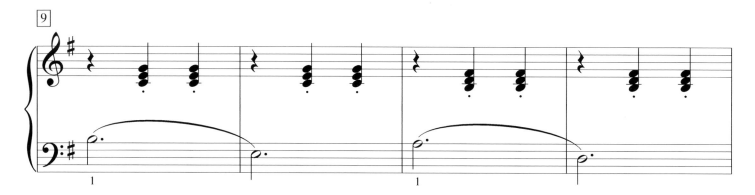

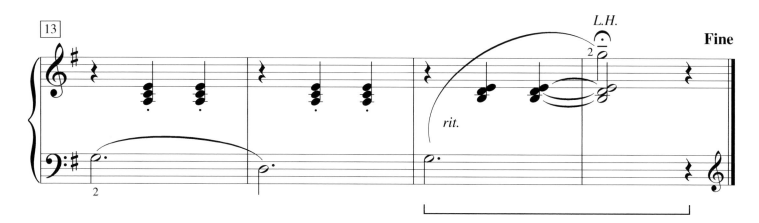

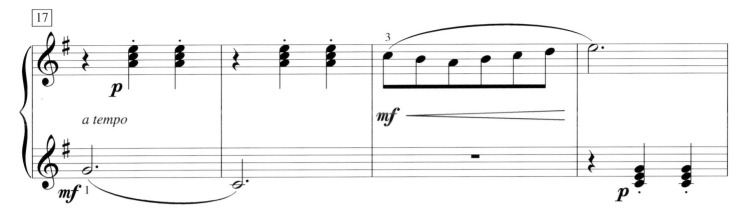

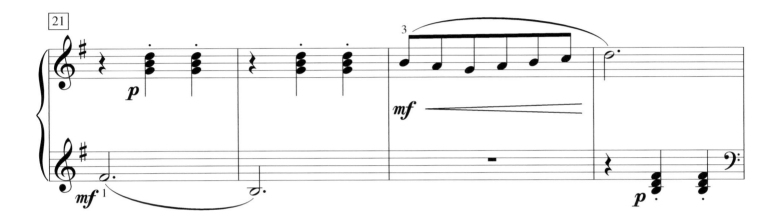

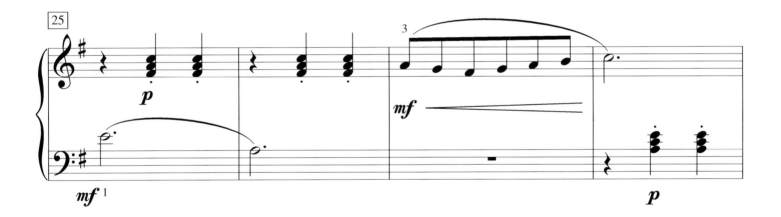

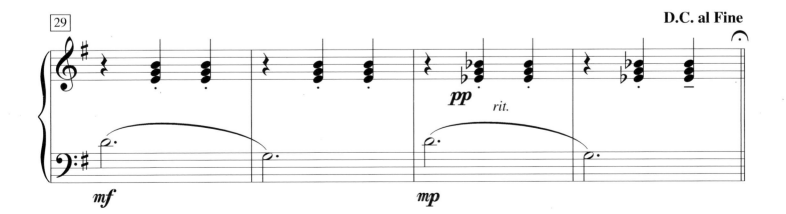

Last Spring

William Gillock

Largo, con poco moto

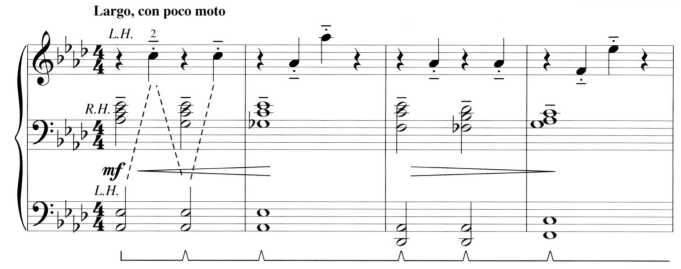

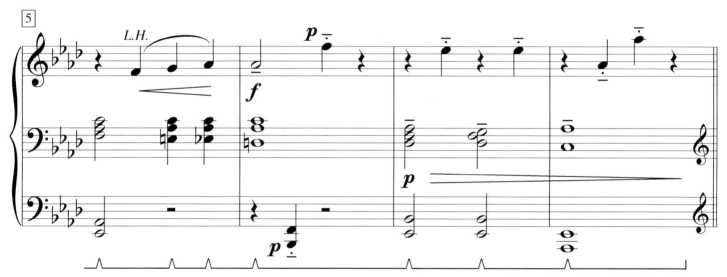

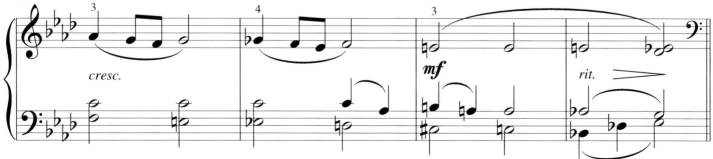

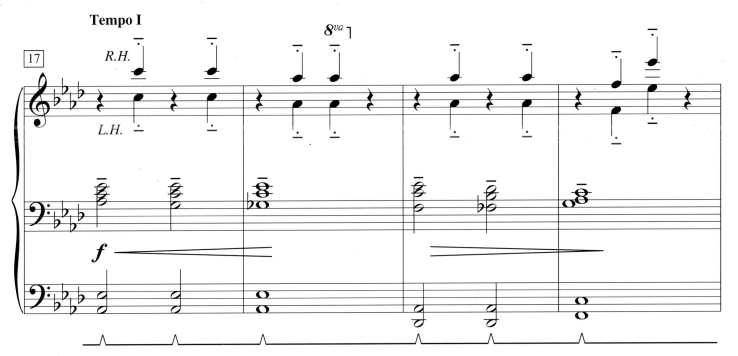

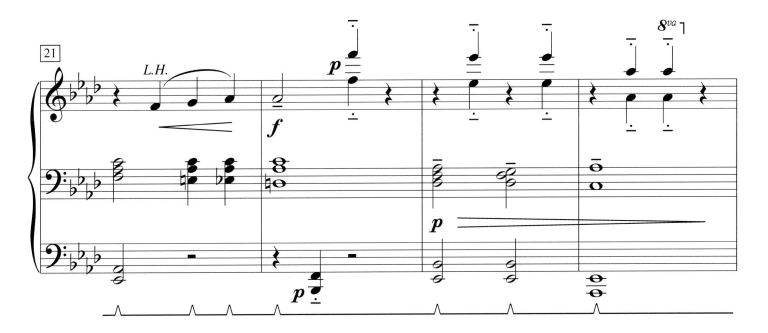

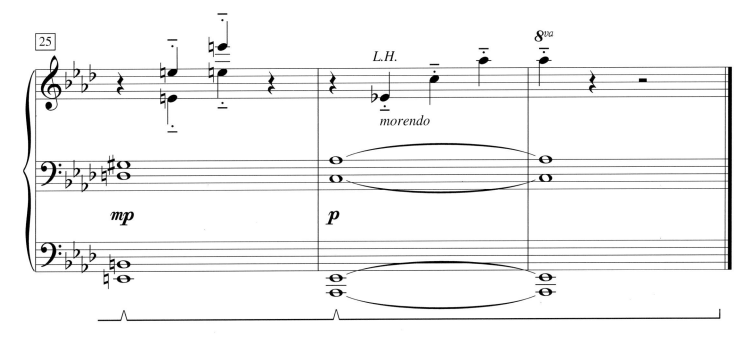

CLASSIC PIANO REPERTOIRE

The *Classic Piano Repertoire* series includes popular as well as lesser-known pieces from a select group of composers out of the Willis piano archives. Every piece has been newly engraved and edited with the aim to preserve each composer's original intent and musical purpose.

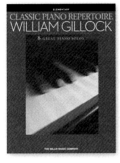

WILLIAM GILLOCK - ELEMENTARY

8 Great Piano Solos

Dance in Ancient Style • Little Flower Girl of Paris • On a Paris Boulevard • Rocking Chair Blues • Sliding in the Snow • Spooky Footsteps • A Stately Sarabande • Stormy Weather.

00416957 ....$8.99

EDNA MAE BURNAM - ELEMENTARY

8 Great Piano Solos

The Clock That Stopped • The Friendly Spider • A Haunted House • New Shoes • The Ride of Paul Revere • The Singing Cello • The Singing Mermaid • Two Birds in a Tree.

00110228 ....$8.99

JOHN THOMPSON - ELEMENTARY

9 Great Piano Solos

Captain Kidd • Drowsy Moon • Dutch Dance • Forest Dawn • Humoresque • Southern Shuffle • Tiptoe • Toy Ships • Up in the Air.

00111968 ....$8.99

LYNN FREEMAN OLSON - EARLY TO LATER ELEMENTARY

14 Great Piano Solos

Caravan • Carillon • Come Out! Come Out! (Wherever You Are) • Halloween Dance • Johnny, Get Your Hair Cut! • Jumping the Hurdles • Monkey on a Stick • Peter the Pumpkin Eater • Pony Running Free • Silent Shadows • The Sunshine Song • Tall Pagoda • Tubas and Trumpets • Winter's Chocolatier.

00294722 ....$9.99

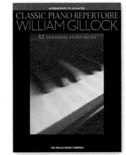

WILLIAM GILLOCK - INTERMEDIATE TO ADVANCED

12 Exquisite Piano Solos

Classic Carnival • Etude in A Major (The Coral Sea) • Etude in E Minor • Etude in G Major (Toboggan Ride) • Festive Piece • A Memory of Vienna • Nocturne • Polynesian Nocturne • Sonatina in Classic Style • Sonatine • Sunset • Valse Etude.

00416912 ....$12.99

EDNA MAE BURNAM - INTERMEDIATE TO ADVANCED

13 Memorable Piano Solos

Butterfly Time • Echoes of Gypsies • Hawaiian Leis • Jubilee! • Longing for Scotland • Lovely Senorita • The Mighty Amazon River • Rumbling Rumba • The Singing Fountain • Song of the Prairie • Storm in the Night • Tempo Tarantelle • The White Cliffs of Dover.

00110229 ....$12.99

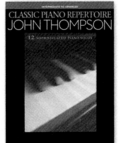

JOHN THOMPSON - INTERMEDIATE TO ADVANCED

12 Masterful Piano Solos

Andantino (from Concerto in D Minor) • The Coquette • The Faun • The Juggler • Lagoon • Lofty Peaks • Nocturne • Rhapsody Hongroise • Scherzando in G Major • Tango Carioca • Valse Burlesque • Valse Chromatique.

00111969 ....$12.99

LYNN FREEMAN OLSON - EARLY TO MID-INTERMEDIATE

13 Distinctive Piano Solos

Band Wagon • Brazilian Holiday • Cloud Paintings • Fanfare • The Flying Ship • Heroic Event • In 1492 • Italian Street Singer • Mexican Serenade • Pageant Dance • Rather Blue • Theme and Variations • Whirlwind.

00294720 ....$9.99

Beloved composer William Lawson Gillock was born in La Russell, Missouri on July 1, 1917. His father, a dentist, was also a musician who played by ear, and undoubtedly influenced his son's love for the piano. There was no piano teacher in the little town of La Russell, and at age 6, Gillock began weekly piano lessons 15 miles away—an extensive distance in the 1920s. Nevertheless, when he went to college, he was hesitant about pursuing a career in music and instead pursued and obtained a degree in art from Central Methodist College. However, his piano and composition teacher at CMC, Dr. N. Louise Wright, recognized his talents and encouraged him to write piano literature specifically for children. Thankfully, he took this advice and thus began his illustrious career as a composer.

Gillock moved to New Orleans in 1943, and the distinctive Southern city would inspire many compositions, including his popular *New Orleans Jazz Styles* books. Gillock also gained respect as a teacher during his tenure in Louisiana, maintaining a studio for almost 30 years. He moved to Dallas, Texas in 1970 where he remained in high demand as a clinician, adjudicator, and composer until his death in 1993.

Affectionately called "the Schubert of children's composers" in tribute to his extraordinary melodic gift, Gillock's numerous piano solos and ensembles exude a special warmth and sophistication. William Gillock was honored on multiple occasions by the National Federation of Music Clubs (NFMC) with the Award of Merit for Service to American Music, and he lives on through his music, which remains immensely popular in the United States, Canada, Japan, and throughout the world.